ITZHAK
A Boy Who Loved the Violin

BY
Tracy Newman

PICTURES BY
Abigail Halpin

Abrams Books for Young Readers • New York

The Perlmans' tiny apartment
seemed ordinary . . .
a single-room walk-up, with just one
window, looking out onto the traffic of
downtown Tel Aviv, and no bathroom of its own.

Yet a little kitchen radio
transformed this simple home.

Graceful classical symphonies,

lively klezmer folk tunes,

soulful cantorial chants,

rich melodies, and
vibrant rhythms

filled this home and the
ears and soul of the
littlest Perlman,

transforming baby
Itzhak, too.

When Itzhak listened to music,
a vivid rainbow of colors appeared in his mind—
hues from dark green to red to yellow.
Music brought Itzhak intense joy. And tears.
Itzhak loved it.
By three, Itzhak knew—he wanted more.
He had to make music.
Young Itzhak had already chosen the instrument
whose magical sound he loved best.
He begged his parents for a violin.
But for an immigrant family whose dinner was
often a piece of watermelon and some bread,
musical instruments were a luxury.
Still Itzhak pestered and pleaded.
Finally, his parents bought him a toy violin.

At first little Itzhak laughed with delight.
But he quickly recognized that his violin
didn't sound like those the master
violinists played.

His music wasn't as

clear

as Jascha Heifetz's,

as intense

as Isaac Stern's,

or as **enchanting** as Ida Haendel's.

Disappointed, Itzhak "gave it a whack and threw it under the bed."

Then the unthinkable happened.
Polio swept through Israel.
Four-year-old Itzhak became infected
with this deadly disease.
He lay hospitalized, fighting for his life.

After a few weeks the doctor announced
that Itzhak was going to live.

But Itzhak's body was weak.
He couldn't move his arms or legs.
At least he could go home.

There were so many tasks to relearn:
    raising his arms over his head,
    holding a book,
    grasping a pencil.
The work was hard, slow, painful.
Other four-year-olds might have given up.
They might have said no.
They might have stopped trying.
But a steady melody played inside Itzhak,
encouraging, energizing, empowering him.

A year of stretching, straightening,
and strengthening paid off.
Itzhak could move his hands and arms again.
But his legs remained paralyzed.
Itzhak would always need crutches or braces to walk.

Crutches or not, Itzhak didn't just sit in his room.
His family moved to the suburbs,
enabling Itzhak to get to school on his own.
They chose an apartment without stairs,
so Itzhak could move around easily.
Crutches even helped his soccer game.
To Itzhak these adjustments were no big deal.
"When you're four years old . . .
you get used to things very, very quickly."

Running around the block,
riding a bicycle,
jumping off a diving board—
all these ordinary things Itzhak would never be able to do.
But Itzhak made an extraordinary choice—
he didn't become sad or angry.
He knew the melody inside him gave him a different gift.
Music got in his ears, gave him goose bumps, sent a chill
through his body.

Recognizing his passion, Itzhak's parents
bought him a new violin.
Crutches meant Itzhak couldn't stand like
most violinists. But Itzhak declared,
"I don't have to play it standing up. I can play
it sitting down . . . "

A bigger challenge was his big fingers—
fitting them into the small spaces
between the strings.

Still, he figured out where
to place them.

Itzhak began studying the violin with a strict
and old-fashioned teacher.
"Do what I tell you. Don't ask any questions," she said.

Itzhak had to practice for two
or three hours every day.
Making music filled Itzhak with joy.
But practicing didn't.

So Itzhak found some unusual ways to manage.
Sometimes he would sneak outside, watching construction trucks pour concrete.
Other times he *boing! boing! boing*ed his bow on the strings, only pretending to play.
If his parents asked why the room was so quiet, Itzhak explained that he was
perfecting a new method—practicing inside his head.

Yet young Itzhak developed exceptional skills,
including his . . .

brilliantly bouncy

SPICCATO

vivid, varied

VIBRATO

speedy
STACCATO
strokes

playful
PIZZICATO
plucking

pizz.

smooth, slow
LEGATO

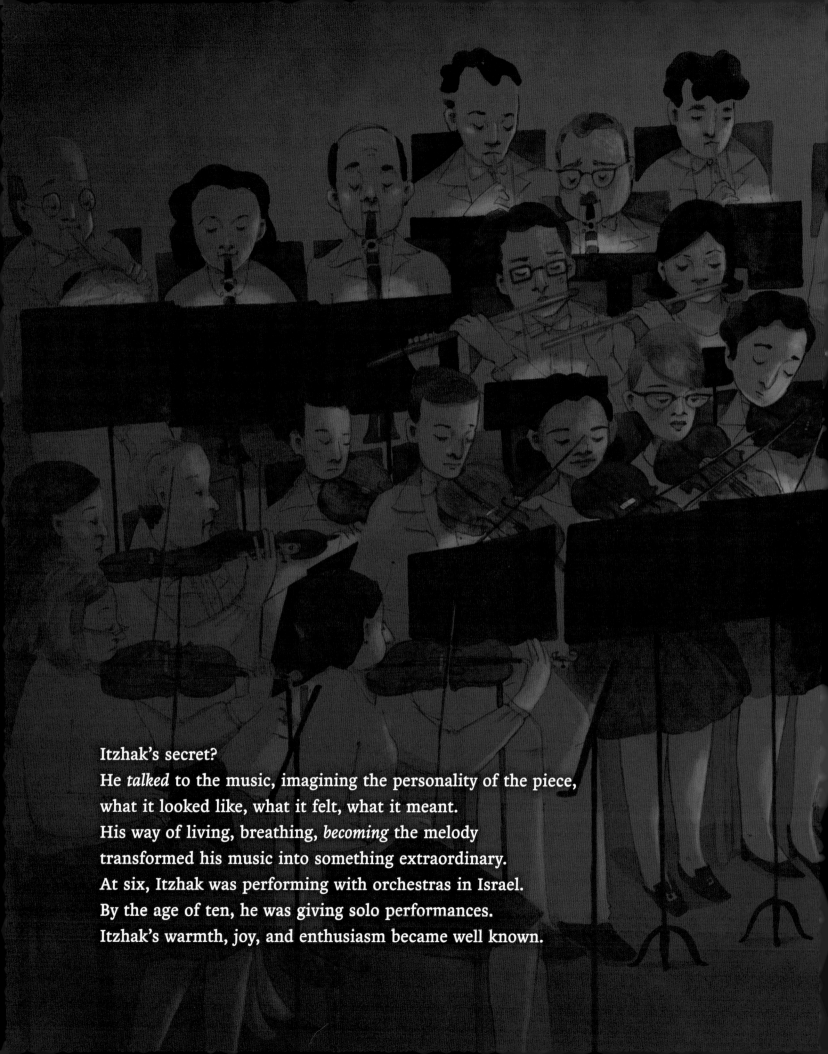

Itzhak's secret?
He *talked* to the music, imagining the personality of the piece,
what it looked like, what it felt, what it meant.
His way of living, breathing, *becoming* the melody
transformed his music into something extraordinary.
At six, Itzhak was performing with orchestras in Israel.
By the age of ten, he was giving solo performances.
Itzhak's warmth, joy, and enthusiasm became well known.

Some people doubted that a violinist could play well sitting down.
Itzhak knew he could.
Later he explained, "I can't walk very well, but I'm not onstage
to do walking. I'm on the stage to play."
Obstacles were ordinary things Itzhak just had to get used to.
But the irresistible melodies vibrating inside his mind
propelled and fortified him.
And so he refused to give up.
At eleven he wrote to the national symphonic orchestra,
the Israel Philharmonic:

I hereby request that you give me an audition
to play. I have the following pieces ready.
Please answer as soon as possible.

Sincerely,
Itzhak Perlman

Itzhak waited and waited,
but the Philharmonic never responded.

MR SULLIVAN

Then came an extraordinary opportunity.
The world-famous variety television show host, Ed Sullivan, whose
show was watched by millions of families each week, traveled to Israel.
Mr. Sullivan was looking for new acts.
So Itzhak auditioned.

Itzhak later admitted that he "played pretty well" for Mr. Sullivan.
Mr. Sullivan agreed.
He invited Itzhak to come to the United States and perform on his show.
Knowing just four words of English—*mother*, *father*, and *good morning*—
thirteen-year-old Itzhak boarded a plane with his mother for New York City.

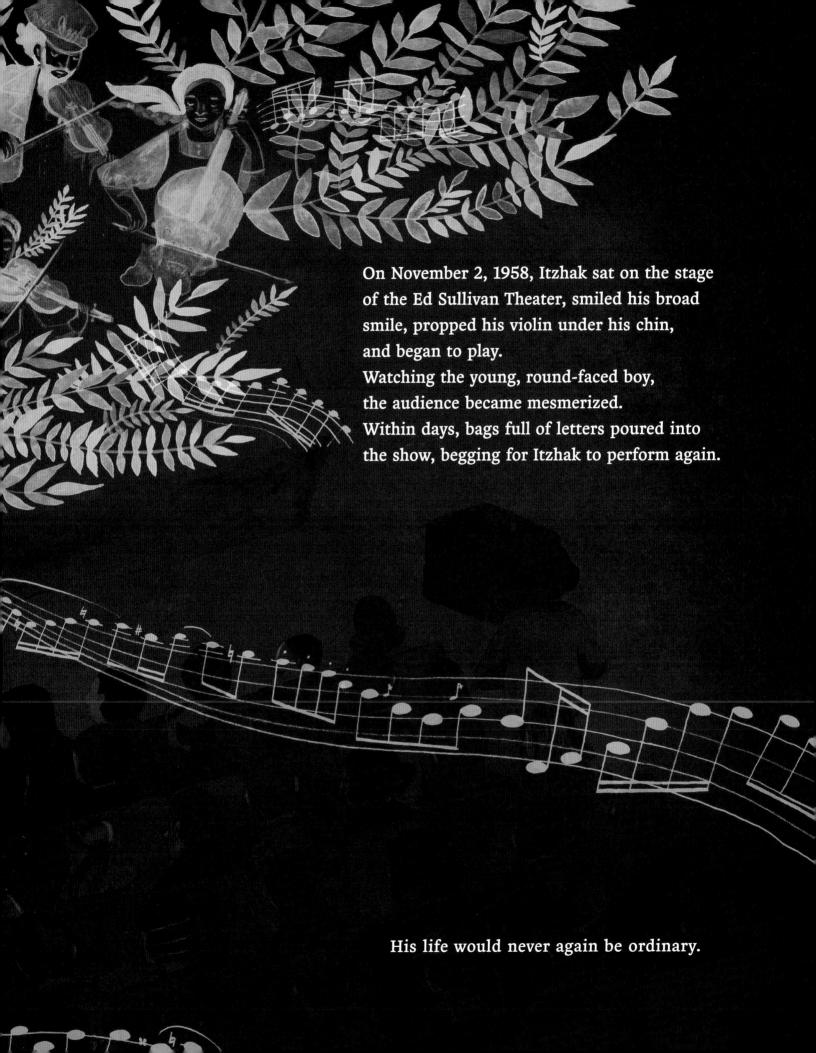

On November 2, 1958, Itzhak sat on the stage
of the Ed Sullivan Theater, smiled his broad
smile, propped his violin under his chin,
and began to play.
Watching the young, round-faced boy,
the audience became mesmerized.
Within days, bags full of letters poured into
the show, begging for Itzhak to perform again.

His life would never again be ordinary.

AUTHOR'S NOTE

Itzhak performed on *The Ed Sullivan Show* five more times and, together with an Israeli magician and a hand-shadow artist, joined Ed Sullivan's *Cavalcade of Stars* on a two-month tour of the United States.

Recognizing Itzhak's talent and passion, the America-Israel Cultural Foundation offered him a scholarship to live in the United States and study music. Itzhak enrolled at the Juilliard School of Music and began studying with master violin teachers.

His hard work continued and grew in many new ways—learning English, adjusting to a new country and to a large and unfamiliar city. Help came from Itzhak's teachers who nurtured the young man and his gift. "What set Itzhak apart from the beginning was his sheer talent and enormous imagination. Itzhak was on a kind of creative high that has never let up."

Itzhak thrived at Juilliard. After graduating, he went on to win the Leventritt Competition, a prestigious international violin competition. The prize was one thousand dollars, professional representation, and the chance to perform for six orchestras across the United States.

Both audiences and critics realized Itzhak's violin playing was extraordinary.

When he was just twenty-four, the *New York Times* declared, "It would be difficult to name half a dozen violinists of any age anywhere who are his equals in both virtuosity and artistry."

Even so, the challenges continued.

"[W]hen it was time to have a career, then people had questions. They had to prove that the quality of what I had to offer was of the highest level." And to develop an international reputation for his violin playing, Itzhak had to travel the world. On crutches.

Performing in concert halls that lacked ramps or elevators was a frequent challenge. Itzhak admitted, "It's like they're telling you, 'Here are our stairs, and you're not welcome here.'" Still Itzhak remained determined to demonstrate that he was capable of being a professional musician.

"I know all the freight and garbage elevators in the major music halls of the world. I've stayed in makeshift dressing rooms that had to be built for me because the real dressing room was on the second floor."

Itzhak's firsthand knowledge of the difficulties faced by people with physical disabilities motivated him to make things better. He is dedicated to improving access to public buildings, including hotels, airports, and concert halls. "It's not a hobby that I happen to do when I'm not playing violin," he says of his championing of the handicapped. "It's part of what my life is about."

Itzhak is also an advocate for children with special needs. He serves on the boards of hospitals for disabled children both in the United States and in Israel, visits wheelchair-bound children, and plays benefit concerts in the wards. In addition, he has appeared on television shows such as *Sesame Street* using his crutches.

Invited to perform with the country's and world's best orchestras, Itzhak has proven himself to be a world-class violinist. In 1967, he recorded his first two albums. He received the first of sixteen Grammy Awards in 1971. In addition, television documentaries recorded several of Itzhak's international concerts, which went on to receive Emmy Awards.

Itzhak's charisma, talent, and good nature helped spread his fame beyond the classical music world. Besides playing violin, his appearances on dozens of television shows, serving as a product spokesperson, and recording a solo for the Oscar-winning soundtrack of the film *Schindler's List* have all made him an international celebrity.

Three presidents of the United States have honored Itzhak with medals for his accomplishments. He performs, conducts orchestras, and teaches students. Itzhak Perlman is widely considered the world's best violinist.

ILLUSTRATOR'S NOTE

One of my first memories of the violin—and by extension, Itzhak Perlman—was via the children's television program *Sesame Street*. I was mesmerized by his playing and knew that someday I, too, wanted to play the violin. But when I finally did take lessons, I faced the rude discovery (like Itzhak) that the violin is hard to play. Really hard. Like throw-the-violin-under-your-bed hard. The violin in the hands of a beginner squeaks and squawks. It feels confusing and counterintuitive. Completely exasperated, I gave up on the violin after only a year of lessons.

Many years later, as an adult looking for a creative outlet, my mind flitted back to my teenage misadventures with the violin. On a whim, I signed up for lessons. Learning violin as an adult was no easier than it had been as a teenager, but armed with zero expectations and a wonderful teacher, something clicked the second time around. I'm so glad to have given that frustrating, beautiful, intriguing instrument another chance.

In illustrating *Itzhak*, I borrowed from my own experiences with the violin. Throughout the book, I've used excerpts from the Bach Double Violin Concerto (the Concerto for Two Violins in D minor) in many of the illustrations. There is a magical recording of Itzhak Perlman and Isaac Stern performing this piece, which I listened to frequently while illustrating. And because it's a piece I played once at a recital, it gave me a personal connection to the music. I frequently found myself humming the notes as I drew them. I've also included portions of Mendelssohn's Violin Concerto, the piece that Itzhak played on *The Ed Sullivan Show*. The recordings of his performance are an absolute delight to watch; Itzhak's enthusiasm is infectious.

While I chose to illustrate *Itzhak* initially because of my experiences with the violin, that reason was quickly superseded by the inspiration I found entering into Itzhak Perlman's story. I am in awe of Mr. Perlman's talent and determination, inspired by his love of family, and I take hope in the joy his playing brings to so very many. To be able to illustrate that kind of a man's story is an experience for which I am truly grateful.

TIMELINE

August 31, 1945	Itzhak Perlman born in Tel Aviv, Palestine (now Israel)
May 14, 1948	The State of Israel established
1950	Began studying violin with Rivka Goldgart at the Shulamit Conservatory and the Academy of Music in Tel Aviv
November 2, 1958	First appearance on *The Ed Sullivan Show*
1958	Moved to New York to study at the Juilliard School of Music with Ivan Galamian and Dorothy DeLay
1963	Debut at Carnegie Hall
1964	Won the prestigious Leventritt Competition
January 6, 1967	Married violinist Toby Friedlander
1977	Received his first of sixteen Grammy Awards
1986	Awarded a Medal of Liberty by President Ronald Reagan
1992	Awarded his first of four Emmy Awards for Outstanding Classical Program in the Performing Arts for *Perlman in Russia*
1993	Performed as violin soloist for John Williams's Academy Award–winning musical score in Steven Spielberg's movie *Schindler's List*
1994	Began teaching full time at the Perlman Music Program
1999	Began teaching at the Juilliard School of Music
2000	Awarded the National Medal of Arts by President Bill Clinton
2003	Appointed to the Dorothy Richard Starling Chair of Violin Studies at the Juilliard School of Music
2008	Honored with a Grammy Lifetime Achievement Award for excellence in the recording arts
2015	Awarded the Presidential Medal of Freedom by President Barack Obama
2016	Awarded Israel's Genesis Prize Laureate

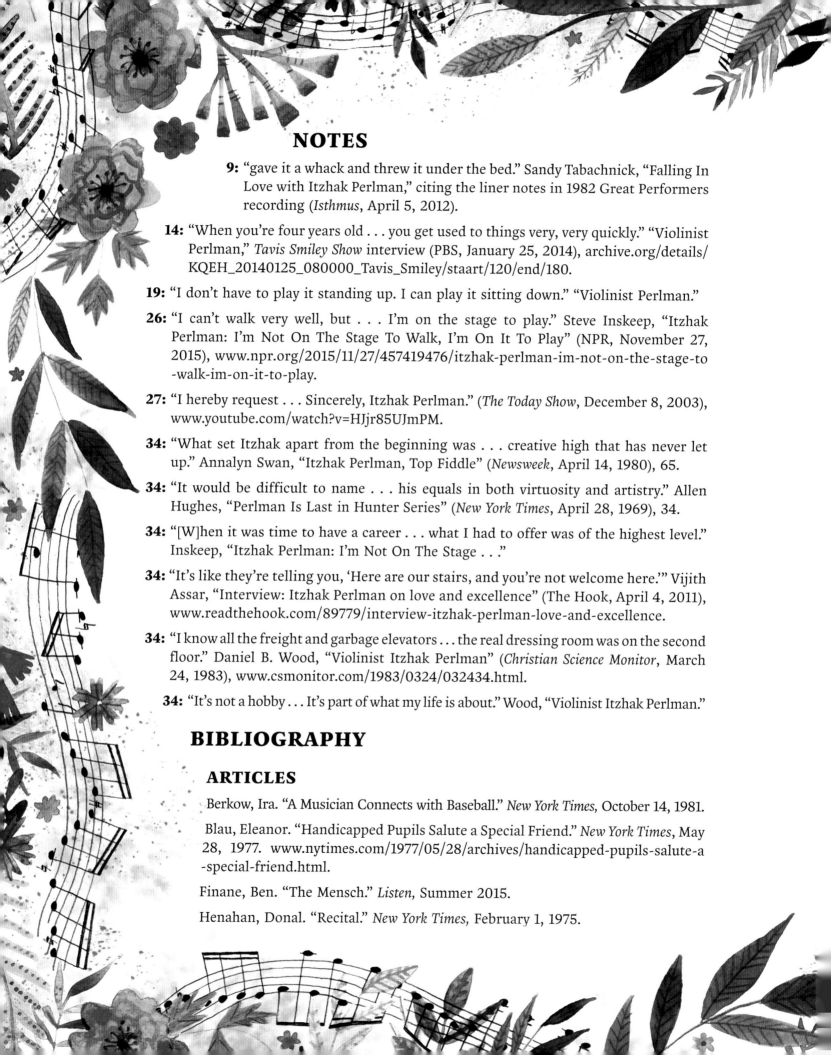

NOTES

9: "gave it a whack and threw it under the bed." Sandy Tabachnick, "Falling In Love with Itzhak Perlman," citing the liner notes in 1982 Great Performers recording (*Isthmus*, April 5, 2012).

14: "When you're four years old . . . you get used to things very, very quickly." "Violinist Perlman," *Tavis Smiley Show* interview (PBS, January 25, 2014), archive.org/details/KQEH_20140125_080000_Tavis_Smiley/staart/120/end/180.

19: "I don't have to play it standing up. I can play it sitting down." "Violinist Perlman."

26: "I can't walk very well, but . . . I'm on the stage to play." Steve Inskeep, "Itzhak Perlman: I'm Not On The Stage To Walk, I'm On It To Play" (NPR, November 27, 2015), www.npr.org/2015/11/27/457419476/itzhak-perlman-im-not-on-the-stage-to-walk-im-on-it-to-play.

27: "I hereby request . . . Sincerely, Itzhak Perlman." (*The Today Show*, December 8, 2003), www.youtube.com/watch?v=HJjr85UJmPM.

34: "What set Itzhak apart from the beginning was . . . creative high that has never let up." Annalyn Swan, "Itzhak Perlman, Top Fiddle" (*Newsweek*, April 14, 1980), 65.

34: "It would be difficult to name . . . his equals in both virtuosity and artistry." Allen Hughes, "Perlman Is Last in Hunter Series" (*New York Times*, April 28, 1969), 34.

34: "[W]hen it was time to have a career . . . what I had to offer was of the highest level." Inskeep, "Itzhak Perlman: I'm Not On The Stage . . ."

34: "It's like they're telling you, 'Here are our stairs, and you're not welcome here.'" Vijith Assar, "Interview: Itzhak Perlman on love and excellence" (The Hook, April 4, 2011), www.readthehook.com/89779/interview-itzhak-perlman-love-and-excellence.

34: "I know all the freight and garbage elevators . . . the real dressing room was on the second floor." Daniel B. Wood, "Violinist Itzhak Perlman" (*Christian Science Monitor*, March 24, 1983), www.csmonitor.com/1983/0324/032434.html.

34: "It's not a hobby . . . It's part of what my life is about." Wood, "Violinist Itzhak Perlman."

BIBLIOGRAPHY

ARTICLES

Berkow, Ira. "A Musician Connects with Baseball." *New York Times,* October 14, 1981.

Blau, Eleanor. "Handicapped Pupils Salute a Special Friend." *New York Times*, May 28, 1977. www.nytimes.com/1977/05/28/archives/handicapped-pupils-salute-a-special-friend.html.

Finane, Ben. "The Mensch." *Listen,* Summer 2015.

Henahan, Donal. "Recital." *New York Times,* February 1, 1975.

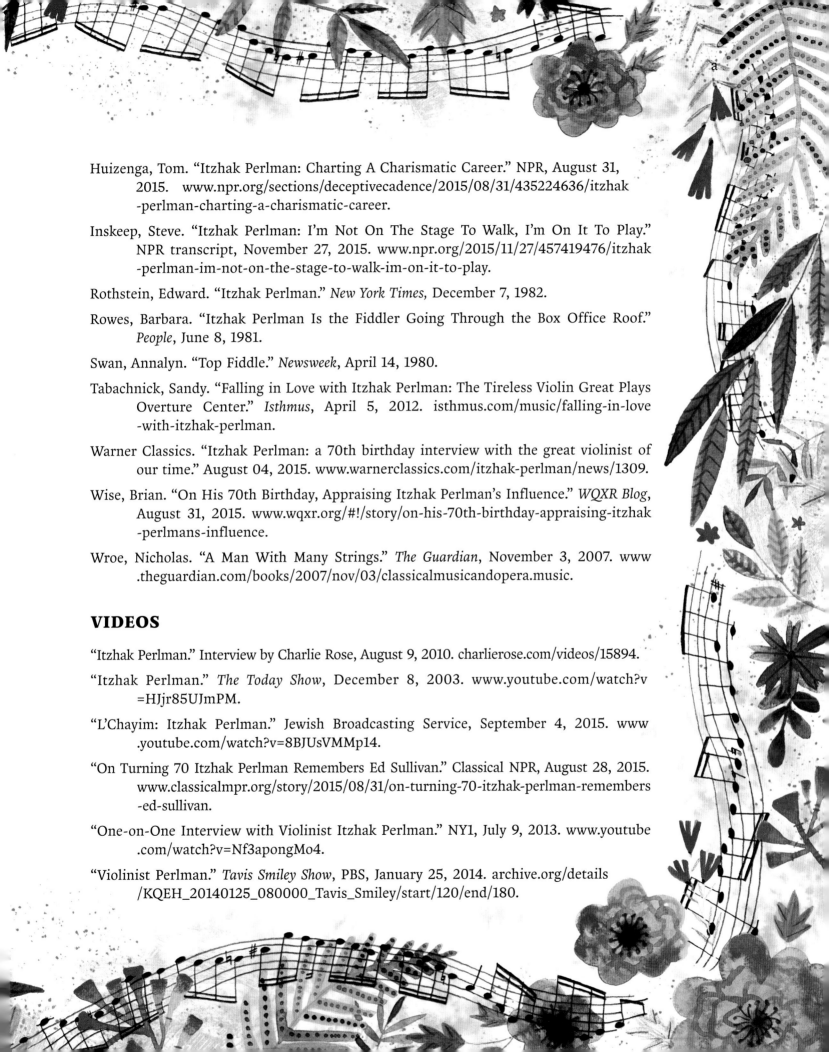

Huizenga, Tom. "Itzhak Perlman: Charting A Charismatic Career." NPR, August 31, 2015. www.npr.org/sections/deceptivecadence/2015/08/31/435224636/itzhak -perlman-charting-a-charismatic-career.

Inskeep, Steve. "Itzhak Perlman: I'm Not On The Stage To Walk, I'm On It To Play." NPR transcript, November 27, 2015. www.npr.org/2015/11/27/457419476/itzhak -perlman-im-not-on-the-stage-to-walk-im-on-it-to-play.

Rothstein, Edward. "Itzhak Perlman." *New York Times,* December 7, 1982.

Rowes, Barbara. "Itzhak Perlman Is the Fiddler Going Through the Box Office Roof." *People*, June 8, 1981.

Swan, Annalyn. "Top Fiddle." *Newsweek*, April 14, 1980.

Tabachnick, Sandy. "Falling in Love with Itzhak Perlman: The Tireless Violin Great Plays Overture Center." *Isthmus*, April 5, 2012. isthmus.com/music/falling-in-love -with-itzhak-perlman.

Warner Classics. "Itzhak Perlman: a 70th birthday interview with the great violinist of our time." August 04, 2015. www.warnerclassics.com/itzhak-perlman/news/1309.

Wise, Brian. "On His 70th Birthday, Appraising Itzhak Perlman's Influence." *WQXR Blog*, August 31, 2015. www.wqxr.org/#!/story/on-his-70th-birthday-appraising-itzhak -perlmans-influence.

Wroe, Nicholas. "A Man With Many Strings." *The Guardian*, November 3, 2007. www .theguardian.com/books/2007/nov/03/classicalmusicandopera.music.

VIDEOS

"Itzhak Perlman." Interview by Charlie Rose, August 9, 2010. charlierose.com/videos/15894.

"Itzhak Perlman." *The Today Show*, December 8, 2003. www.youtube.com/watch?v =HJjr85UJmPM.

"L'Chayim: Itzhak Perlman." Jewish Broadcasting Service, September 4, 2015. www .youtube.com/watch?v=8BJUsVMMp14.

"On Turning 70 Itzhak Perlman Remembers Ed Sullivan." Classical NPR, August 28, 2015. www.classicalmpr.org/story/2015/08/31/on-turning-70-itzhak-perlman-remembers -ed-sullivan.

"One-on-One Interview with Violinist Itzhak Perlman." NY1, July 9, 2013. www.youtube .com/watch?v=Nf3apongMo4.

"Violinist Perlman." *Tavis Smiley Show*, PBS, January 25, 2014. archive.org/details /KQEH_20140125_080000_Tavis_Smiley/start/120/end/180.

To Marc, Benji, and Rose—
my best cheerleaders
— T.N.

For Eloïse
— A.H.

The illustrations in this book were rendered in
watercolor and colored pencil, and finished digitally.

Library of Congress Cataloging-in-Publication Data:

Names: Newman, Tracy, 1971– author. | Halpin, Abigail, illustrator.
Title: Itzhak : a boy who loved the violin / by Tracy Newman ; illustrated by Abigail Halpin.
Description: New York, NY: Abrams Books for Young Readers, 2020.
Identifiers: LCCN 2019010421 | ISBN 9781419741104
Subjects: LCSH: Perlman, Itzhak, 1945– —Juvenile literature. | Violinists—Biography—Juvenile
literature.
Classification: LCC ML3930.P45 N49 2020 | DDC 787.2092 [B]—dc23
ISBN 978-1-4197-4110-4

Text copyright © 2020 Tracy Newman
Illustrations copyright © 2020 Abigail Halpin
Book design by Steph Stilwell

Printed and bound in China
10 9 8 7 6 5 4 3 2 1

Abrams Books for Young Readers are available at special discounts when purchased
in quantity for premiums and promotions as well as fundraising or educational use.
Special editions can also be created to specification. For details, contact
specialsales@abramsbooks.com or the address below.

Abrams® is a registered trademark of Harry N. Abrams, Inc.

ABRAMS The Art of Books
195 Broadway, New York, NY 10007
abramsbooks.com